Lilly Lady Bug
and Her Leaf Blanket

Everything you never knew about trees.

CASEY — MAY YOU HAVE MANY TREE FRIENDS!

Written and Illustrated by

Maurine Frank

Maurine Frank

ISBN: 979-8-853049-41-3

Published by High Tide Publications, Inc.
www.hightidepublications.com

Thank you for purchasing an authorized edition of *Lilly Lady Bug and Her Leaf Blanket.*

High Tide's mission is to find, encourage, promote, and publish the work of authors. We are a small, woman-owned enterprise that is dedicated to the author over 50. When you buy an authorized copy, you help us to bring their work to you.

We thank you for supporting our authors.

Edited by Cindy L. Freeman cindy@cindylfreeman.com

Book Design by Firebellied Frog Graphic Design

www.firebelliedfrog.com

This book is dedicated to Abby Williams, certainly a girly girl, but one who loves ladybugs, trees, and all things in nature.

L illy was a ladybug who loved to snuggle in her little burrow under a beautiful leaf that had a very unusual shape. It wrapped around her perfectly.

On sunny days she would often visit with the dandelions, caterpillars, and bumblebees. She enjoyed the wonderful smell of new grass. Most of all she liked to show off her shiny red coat with the big black dots. Her life was quite nice.

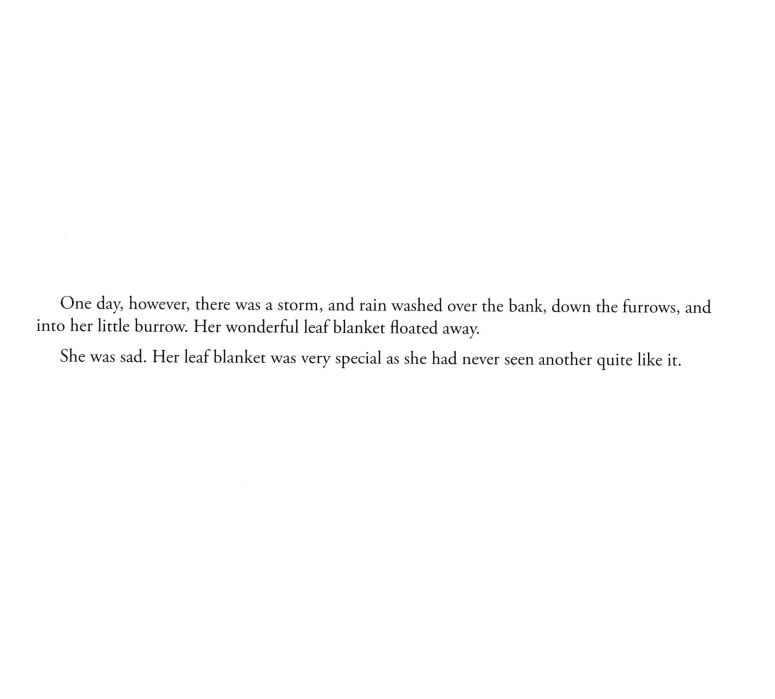

One day, however, there was a storm, and rain washed over the bank, down the furrows, and into her little burrow. Her wonderful leaf blanket floated away.

She was sad. Her leaf blanket was very special as she had never seen another quite like it.

Lilly had many tree friends and thought they might be able to help her find another leaf like the one she had lost. She often talked to them, and they talked among themselves. It's true. Trees *do* talk. If you venture into the woods and are very quiet, you will hear them whispering to each other. We do not understand what they are saying because humans have never taken the time to learn the language of trees, but ladybugs certainly do.

She set off for the forest. She would walk a little bit and she would fly a little bit, and soon she was surrounded by many trees. She flitted up and landed on a branch that belonged to Orville Oak.

"Hi there, Lilly," whispered Orville. "What brings you so deep into the forest today?"

"I am looking for a very special leaf. I need a new blanket."

"I'd be happy to give you one of my leaves," said Orville. He rustled his mighty trunk. Oak trees are often the biggest and tallest trees in the forest. One big leaf came cascading down and settled across the branch where Lilly was sitting.

She checked it out, side to side, top to bottom. Orville was a red oak. The leaf was beautiful, with nice red tips, but it was not the leaf she was looking for. Lilly knew Orville was proud of his leaves, as oaks were among the proudest of trees, and she did not want to seem ungrateful.

"This is a beautiful leaf and would make a nice blanket, but it's a bit too big for me."

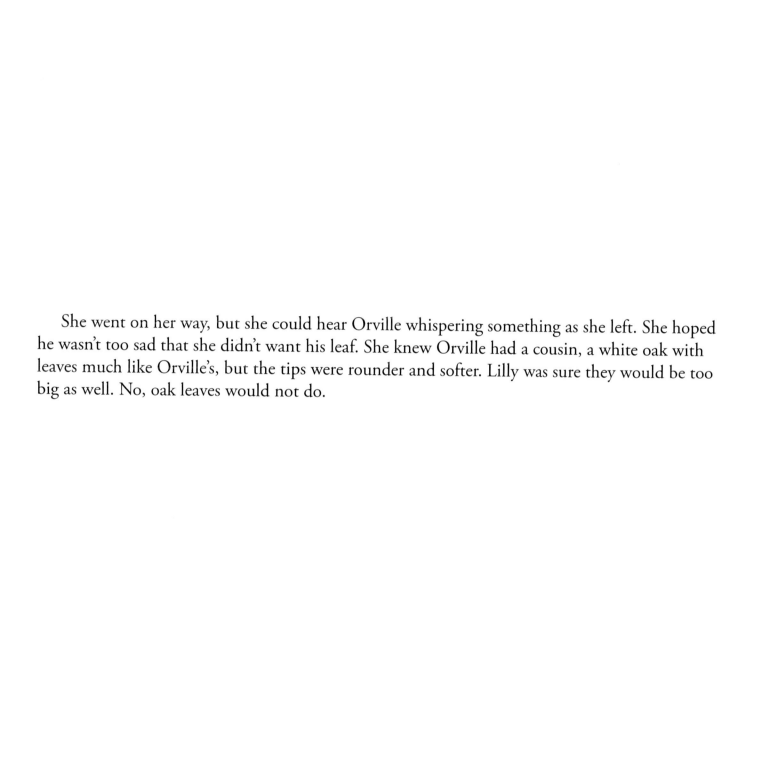

She went on her way, but she could hear Orville whispering something as she left. She hoped he wasn't too sad that she didn't want his leaf. She knew Orville had a cousin, a white oak with leaves much like Orville's, but the tips were rounder and softer. Lilly was sure they would be too big as well. No, oak leaves would not do.

Next, she encountered two smaller trees. She knew these guys did not have leaves but had needles instead. She said "Hi" anyway.

One was Freddie Fir and close by was Stanley Spruce, the evergreen cousins. Humans sometimes get confused as to which is a fir and which is a spruce, but Lilly could easily tell them apart.

Freddie was warm and friendly. His needles were soft. Lilly often nestled in his branches, which were comfortable and welcoming. She could remember he was a fir tree by saying, "Firs are friendly."

Stanley was a bit grumpy. His needles were prickly and not soft or comfortable at all. She could remember Stanley was a spruce tree by saying, "Spruce are scratchy!"

Freddie Fir said, "Hello Lilly. I hope you are having a nice day."

Stanley Spruce said, "Humph!"

Next was Billy Birch. Lilly could see he had some nice leaves. They were soft and flat but still not like her blanket. As Lilly flew by, Billy smiled and waved his branches.

She was looking back and complimenting Billy on his handsome leaves when she flew right into Andy Aspen! Kwhack! She rubbed her head and laughed, and Andy laughed as well. The sun was brightly bouncing off his leaves, and Lilly thought perhaps the sun was laughing too. Her bumping into Andy had been a funny sight!

He was one of her best, but most peculiar, friends. First, Andy always stood straight and tall. His trunk was not brown and covered with bark at all. Instead, it was white and smooth. His leaves, which were too small for a blanket, were attached to his branches with long, thin stems and when the wind blew, his stems twisted and quaked, which sounded to Lilly like laughter.

Andy was always fun to be around. He had once told her a secret. "Under the ground, my roots are connected to all the other aspens in this grove. We look like many trees, but actually we are all one big tree."

Lilly explained what had happened to her blanket. Andy suggested she check out Maggie Maple's leaves. "I think they'd make the perfect replacement. Maggie is just down the way," he said.

Lilly made her way deeper into the forest. Humans were often afraid of going too far into the woods. She thought perhaps it was because they had not gotten to know the trees as she had. Sometimes humans do not realize how incredibly helpful trees are. Not only do they freely provide shade, food, and shelter, but trees supply the oxygen that humans need to breathe. Humans could not exist without trees. Lilly knew this only too well. In addition to being helpful, trees are incredibly wise. After all, most trees are quite old and have spent many years standing still and watching and listening.

Lilly had heard that some trees in a place called California are between 4,000 and 5,000 years old! Those trees must surely know everything. Lilly knew one thing. She needed to find her blanket before winter came, so she traveled on.

She was thinking very hard about trees and how they often warn each other of danger and could offer directions to anyone who might be lost. She knew that moss only grows on the cooler north side of her tree friends, which is a good guide when Lilly is going south. She was thinking so hard that she tumbled right over a branch belonging to Edith Elm.

"Ouch!" she said and checked her beautiful red coat to make sure none of her dots had been damaged.

Edith whispered, "Sorry about that, but after all I was here first!"

Lilly was fine, just a little dazed.

"I know," she replied. "I was deep in thought about how helpful trees are, and I wasn't watching where I was going."

Edith Elm's leaves swished this way and that as she laughed.

"Well, I certainly helped get your attention! What else can I help you with?"

Lilly explained she was looking for a particular leaf. Edith's leaves were a beautiful shape, but again not the right fit. Her best hope was to find Maggie Maple. She didn't want to hurt Edith's feelings, so she reminded her how helpful her leaves had been when Lilly wanted to float across puddles after a rain. They made perfect boats! Edith beamed with pride, and she flitted a leaf or two down to the ground in case they might be needed.

Maggie was Lilly's last hope. However, she had heard that Maggie was a silver maple and was quite stuck-up. She found that a little funny because Maggie's cousins supplied sticky sap that made delicious maple syrup, and she thought if anyone should be stuck-up it should be them! That seemed so funny to her that she giggled and giggled. Soon she was laughing so hard she flew right past Maggie without noticing.

Lilly looked back to see Maggie turning her leaves in the breeze to catch their shiny, silver underside. As the sun bounced off them, they glittered and danced. Maggie held her head in a haughty manner. Her leaves were quite remarkable, and Lilly could understand why Maggie was so proud. She also could see that, although sleeping under such a fancy blanket might be impressive, Maggie did not have the leaf Lilly was after.

What was she to do? Where had her blanket come from? She had checked out almost all the trees in the forest. She really missed her blanket and had so wanted to find another.

Just then, not far away, was a funny little tree she had hardly noticed. What a surprise! There were her leaves. Lilly was so excited she flew over making loop-de-loops and landed on one of the branches. She hopped on a leaf and wrapped it around her. It fit perfectly and was ever so comfortable.

The little tree looked at her.

"Um, excuse me," said Lilly. "I don't think we've met."

The little tree just gave Lilly the side-eye and did not say a word.

Lilly explained about her lost blanket and politely asked if she might have a leaf for a replacement. The tree glared at her, then puckered up and let loose with a whirlwind response. "Excuse me? Excuse me? I'll excuse you, young lady! You come here and dare, AND DARE ask for one of my leaves?"

Lilly noticed that most of her tree friends talked in gentle whispers, but this tree spoke quite shrilly.

"I'll tell you a thing or two! I am constantly expected to give up my bark for tea and my roots for root beer! Now here you are asking for leaves. What next! I'll tell you what next…."

This tree went on and on fussing about everything from the birds to the weather.

Wow, Lilly thought. *What have I gotten myself into?*

Then she realized this was a sassafras tree. Of course! Why wouldn't a sassafras tree be sassy? That was to be expected. She had heard tales about Sam Sassafras but had never had the pleasure of meeting him—if one could call meeting such a sassy tree a pleasure. He sassed everything and everyone at every opportunity. And he was good at it. However, Lilly had also been told that once you got to know Sam, he did have a good side. He could be very generous.

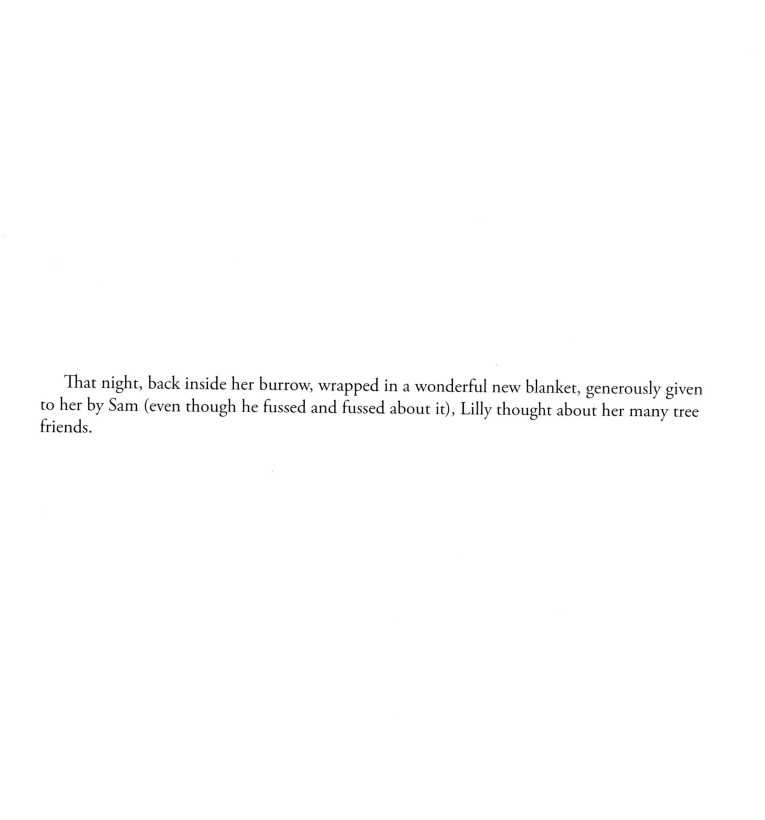

That night, back inside her burrow, wrapped in a wonderful new blanket, generously given to her by Sam (even though he fussed and fussed about it), Lilly thought about her many tree friends.

Trees are interesting, she mused. *Each tree is different in size and appearance but still they are similar. Each has its own personality, set of leaves, and distinct way. Some are proud and show-offs. Some are peaceful and comforting, others a bit hard to like and somewhat grumpy, but each one is valuable, and special, with a generous and helpful side. Even Sam, sassy and not so pleasant, is willing to help.*

Yep, she thought, as she drifted off to sleep. *Yep, trees are special friends. They are helpful and wise. Even in winter, when they let go of their precious leaves and find themselves bare and vulnerable, they still stand confidently. They remain steadfast and never worry. They stretch their bare branches before the cold wind with self-assurance, because they know that spring, and better days, and new growth, will always return.*

And come to think of it…don't you think trees are a bit like people? All different, but all the same. Some are wise, some fun, and others grumpy, but even the grumpy ones can have a kind side. And don't you think we could all take a lesson from trees? Stand tall and strong and have confidence that, no matter what, spring and better days will always return? Yes, we could all learn a thing or two from trees.

The End

About Lilly and Her Tree Friends

The next time you see a tree, or take a walk in the woods, you can recognize Lilly's friends by looking at their leaves. You can tell a spruce from a fir by feeling their needles. You can tell an aspen from the other trees by looking at their leaves or their bark. As you walk along, listen to the sounds that trees make. They rustle their leaves and scrape their branches together. Do you think they are talking to each other? Or to you? Perhaps they are trying to tell their story. Maybe they are asking you a question. It is always fun to imagine what tales a tree that has lived in the same spot for hundreds of years might tell you if only you could understand.

Lilly knows many interesting things about her tree friends, but there are things that you might like to know as well.

Did you know….

- Trees are plants. They are the largest and longest living plants on the planet!

- Trees come from a very large family with so many cousins you couldn't count them all! There are almost 60,000 different types of trees on Earth.

- Some of the largest trees, called sequoias, are found in California. One of them was measured at over 367 feet tall. (How tall are you?) You would look very small standing beside such a large tree. Lilly would look even smaller!

- Trees provide homes for thousands of animals, birds, and bugs. Ladybugs too!

- Trees are very helpful with their wood. Many of our houses are made of wood, as are boats, furniture, and some playgrounds. What other things can you think of that are made from wood?

- Many people think that leaves fall off a tree in the cooler season, but the trees decide when their leaves need to go. Winter months can be windy, and wind against broad flat leaves could cause a lot of damage. So could heavy snow. Trees protect themselves by letting their leaves fall to the ground. Aren't they smart!

- Why are leaves green? It is because they have chlorophyl in them which allows them to soak up the sunlight and turn it into food for the tree. Chlorophyl is big word! It is pronounced *clor-o-fill*.

- When the days become shorter with less sunlight, the production of green chlorophyl slows down until it finally stops. As the green goes away, other colors that were hidden in the leaf begin to show. Those colors can be red, yellow, orange, or even purple.

- What about Freddie Fir and Stanley Spruce? Why don't they shed their needles? Evergreens hang on to their needles because they are coated in wax which protects them from snow and cold.

- Why are trees so important to us? Trees remove carbon dioxide from the air. Carbon dioxide is poisonous to us humans. Trees replace it with oxygen, which humans need to breathe. The fact is…no person or animal could survive without trees! That is why it is good to get to know them and make them our friends. And we should be good friends to them too.

Some very official information about Lilly's tree friends…

- **OAK** – An oak is in the Beech family. There are five hundred species of oaks. It is native to the northern hemisphere and one of the most common trees in North America. There are two major types: red oak and white oak.

- **FIR** – Firs are evergreen or coniferous trees which are an important source of softwood and supply resins and turpentine. There are more than forty species found throughout North and Central America. They are also in Europe, Asia, and North Africa. The tallest firs can reach heights of 260 feet. They have needle-like leaves that stay green all year.

- **SPRUCE** - Spruce are also evergreen coniferous trees. There are about thirty-five species found in the northern regions of the earth. Spruce are large trees from 60 to 200 feet when mature. They have whorled branches that are a conical shape which are four-sided and attached to a small peg-like structure on a branch. In the mountains of western Sweden there is a spruce tree that has reached the age of 9,550 years and is thought to be the world's oldest living tree.

- **BIRCH** – Birch is a deciduous tree with about forty species and lives throughout the cooler regions of the Northern Hemisphere. Birch trees have papery bark. The wood of a birch has been used for birchbark canoes and the bark used for making baskets. They can grow from 60 to 100 feet tall.

- **ASPEN** – Aspens live in the cooler regions of the Northern Hemisphere but are also found in southern areas that have high altitudes. They are deciduous and can reach up to 100 feet tall. They are often called Quaking Aspen because their leaves have flattened petioles (stalks) and seem to quake in the wind. Most aspens are found in large colonies derived from a single seedling that has spread by way of root suckers.

- **ELM** – The American Elm is a deciduous tree found throughout Southern Canada and the United States, particularly in the Eastern regions. It can grow up to 100 feet tall. Its bark is deeply furrowed and light-to-dark gray in color.

- **MAPLE** – The maple is a deciduous tree. There are about 130 different species. The sap from maples can be made into syrup. They can grow from 20 to 80 feet in height. They are found throughout Asia and North America. Their bark is brown and smooth when they are young but becomes rough and ridged as the tree matures.

- **SASSAFRASS** – The sassafras is a deciduous tree. It is native to Asia and North America. They can be from thirty to sixty feet tall. Sassafrass are distinguished by their aromatic properties. Their leaves can have a distinctive right- and left-handed mitten shape. Their bark is an attractive red-brown color when they are young and gradually develops interlacing furrows and ridges as they mature.

Some big words you might like to have explained…

Deciduous - A tree that sheds its leaves every year.

Coniferous - A tree that has cones (like pinecones). It has needle-like or scale-like leaves that are usually evergreen.

Species - A group of similar living things that share common characteristics.

Hemisphere - A half-portion of the earth, usually divided into the north and south halves by the equator, or the eastern and western halves divided by an imaginary line from the North Pole to the South Pole.

Altitude - How high something is. It usually refers to the atmosphere.

Conical - A circular shape with a wider base at one end and a point at the other; cone-shaped.

Petiole - A stalk that attaches the leaf blade to its stem.

Root suckers - Shoots springing from the roots of a plant or a tree.

Aromatic - A pleasant or distinctive smell.

And another big word and perhaps the most important of all…

Psithurism (pronounced *sith-oo-rih-sum*) – The sound that trees make when the wind blows through their leaves and branches. Or better still…tree language.

If we only knew how to speak psithurism…

Fir Needles

This is a fir sprig. Fir trees have needles instead of leaves. They are waxy green and do not change color in the fall. They stay green all year.

Elm Leaf

This is an elm leaf. It is green in summer and when fall comes, it turns to a yellowish brown.

Spruce Needles

This is a spruce sprig. Spruce trees do not have leaves. They have needles. These are usually a waxy green color or can be a greenish-blue color. They do not change color in winter but keep their same color all year.

White Oak Leaf

This is a white oak leaf. In the fall, the white oak leaves turn deep purple until freezing temperatures, and then they turn brown. White oak leaves are green in the summer.

Aspen Leaf

This is an aspen leaf. In summer they are a light, bright, almost lime-green color. In fall the aspen leaf turns a brilliant yellow gold.

Red Oak Leaf

This is a red oak leaf. It is green in the summer. They can be from orange to a bright, very deep red in the fall.

Birch Leaf

This is a birch leaf. It is glossy green in summer but will turn to gold and yellow colors in the fall.

This is a maple leaf. It is green in summer. The silver maple is also green, but the underside of the leaf is a light greenish-silver color. In fall, maple leaves can change to several brilliant colors. They can turn gold, orange, purple, or a bright red and can be the most beautifully colored trees of all when cooler weather comes.

Maple Leaf

Sassafras Leaf

This is a sassafras leaf. It is bright to medium green in summer and can have three different shapes, including a mitten shape. In fall, these leaves change to a beautiful red, deep orange, yellow, scarlet, or purple.

Fun Things to Do with Leaves!

Save a Leaf

Find a beautiful leaf and place it between two pieces of paper towel. Lay this inside a heavy book, close the book, and put it away for a couple of weeks. When you get it out, you will have a beautiful, perfectly preserved leaf to save. Perhaps it is a memento of a fun vacation, or a special place you visited. You could write a little story about this leaf.

Leaf Painting

You'll need craft paper and craft paint. Take a walk in the woods and find some fallen leaves with interesting shapes. Then paint on them using lots of different colors. While the paint is still wet, press the leaves down onto some white paper. You'll have a beautiful colored print with a leaf shape. Add other leaf prints with different colors and different designs. Hang your painting on the wall in your room, and each time you see it, you will be reminded of the walk you took.

Make a Leaf Sun-Catcher

You will need a roll of clear contact paper and a piece of twine, ribbon, or string. Leaves are their most colorful in the fall. Find several that are different shapes in brilliant colors: red, purple, orange, yellow, etc. Cut a square from the contact paper a little bigger than you think you will need and arrange the leaves on the sticky side. Then cut another square about the same size as the first. Lay the sticky side down on top of the leaves and press it over and all around the leaves. Sometimes it can be hard to get the two pieces of contact paper to exactly match up, so you can trim the edges to cut off any extra contact paper and make the square the size you want. Now you have a beautiful leaf picture. Punch holes in the top and tie your string through. You can hang your picture in a window. The colorful leaves will catch the sun and perhaps even make interesting leaf-shaped shadows in your room!

Make Your Own Fall Tree Picture

For this project you will need some brown paint, also glue, and craft paper. Lay your arm and hand with your fingers spread out on a piece of white craft paper. Have someone draw a line starting on one side of your arm near the wrist area and up around all your fingers and thumb and back down the other side around your wrist and arm. Now paint the area inside that line brown. Don't you think it looks a bit like a tree trunk with branches? Next, go on a hike and pick up all kinds of leaves: big ones, little ones, and lots of different colors. Glue the leaves onto the branches of the tree you painted. You can even glue some leaves at the bottom of your picture like they have fallen off and are lying on the ground. You will have a beautiful tree picture made from your very own arm and hand!

Make a Leaf Bowl

You will need clay—the kind that dries hard, not modeling clay, and a plastic craft knife, because they are not too sharp. You don't want to cut yourself! You might want some craft paint, too. Find a beautiful leaf. The bigger the better. Sometimes green leaves work better for this project because they don't easily crumble. Roll out your clay into a thin patty that is bigger than your leaf. Put the back side of the leaf on the patty and press your leaf down into the clay until it makes an imprint. It's nice if all the lines and veins on the back of the leaf are pressed into the clay. When you feel sure you have an imprint, take your plastic craft knife, and cut away the clay all around the leaf. Then peel your leaf off the clay. You should have a nice clay leaf. Now push up the edges of the leaf until it forms a small bowl. Move it carefully to a safe place to dry. Once it is completely dry, you can leave it the clay color, or you can paint it. Either way you have a leaf bowl to put in your room to hold tiny treasures!

Author, Maurine Frank, believes it has never been more important to encourage an appreciation and love of nature in young people—both for their benefit and the future of our planet. Screentime for youths is at an all-time high, while outdoor time is at an all-time low, even though studies show that getting kids outside enhances their health and physical well-being, while fostering their imaginations, attention spans, and emotional development. This book introduces kids, in a fun way, to the world of trees and all that they contribute to us. A walk in the woods will never be the same after they have met Lilly and her tree friends. She says, "Let's get kids outside, immersed in their natural environment, to create a lifelong concern and appreciation for this home of ours called Earth."

Other books by Maurine Frank:

I know that every individual is significant and believe that our existence affects countless people in countless ways. I also believe that within each of us is a spark that can be extinguished or can glow based on encouragement from others. I'm convinced that taking pride in our light and using it for good is essential and it begins at an early age. The heart of this work is similar to writing a children's story with a solid moral The moral in **Blue Crab Finds a Home** *is if you care about others and treat them with kindness, you will bring joy into peoples lives and ultimately be supported in doing whatever you put your mind to.*

Made in the USA
Middletown, DE
27 August 2023